WHAT DOES GOD SAY ABOUT TODAY'S LAW ENFORCEMENT OFFICER?

RANDY EMON

Copyright © 2015 by Randy Emon

What Does God Say About Today's Law Enforcement Officer?
What Every Cop Needs to Know
by Randy Emon

Printed in the United States of America.

ISBN 9781498438605

All rights reserved solely by the author. The author guarantees all contents are original and do not infringe upon the legal rights of any other person or work. No part of this book may be reproduced in any form without the permission of the author. The views expressed in this book are not necessarily those of the publisher.

Unless otherwise indicated, Scripture quotations marked (TLB) are taken from The Living Bible, copyright © 1971. Used by permission of Tyndale House Publishers, Inc., Carol Strea, Illinois 60188. All rights reserved.

Scripture quotations marked (NKJV) are taken from the New King James Version®. Copyright © 1982 by Thomas Nelson. Used by permission. All rights reserved.

Scripture quotations marked (ESV) are from the Holy Bible, English Standard Version®, copyright © 2001 by Crossway, a publishing ministry of Good News Publishers. Used by permission. All rights reserved.

Scripture quotations marked (NASB) are taken from the New American Standard Bible®, Copyright © 1960, 1962, 1963, 1968, 1971, 1972, 1973, 1975, 1977, 1995 by The Lockman Foundation. Used by permission. (www.Lockman.org)

Scripture quotations marked (NIV) are taken from the Holy Bible, New International Version®, NIV®. Copyright © 1973, 1978, 1984, 2011 by Biblica, Inc.™ Used by permission of Zondervan. All rights reserved worldwide. www.zondervan.com. The "NIV" and "New International Version" are trademarks registered in the United States Patent and Trademark Office by Biblica, Inc.™

www.xulonpress.com

Dedication

This book is dedicated to my wife, Lora, who has stood by my side for over forty years, enduring the rigors as the wife of a law enforcement officer. This book is also dedicated to my three children, Corey, Chris and Tiffany, who are also serving as law enforcement officers.

Table of Contents

Dedication v

Acknowledgments xi

Introduction xv

Chapter 1

God's Job Description Of The Law Enforcement Officer 17

Chapter 2

How The Bible Permits Law Enforcement Officers To Do Their Job 23

Chapter 3

In What Manner May A Law Enforcement Officer Enforce The Laws? 27

Chapter 4
Does The Bible Give Law Enforcement Officers
Authority To Do Their Job? 31

Chapter 5
The Law Enforcement Officer And The Use Of
Less Lethal Types Of Force. 35

Chapter 6
The Law Enforcement Officer And The Use Of
Deadly Force. 41

Chapter 7
The Law Enforcement Officer – An Occupation Or
A Calling? 45

Chapter 8
Will Every Law Enforcement Officer Automatically
Get Into Heaven? 47

Chapter 9
So, What Does God Really Say About Today's
Law Enforcement Officer?. 49

Table of Contents

Biblical Encouragement For Christian Law Enforcement Officers. 53

Wise Sayings For Cops. 63

A Prayer For Today's Law Enforcement Officer. 69

Appendix 73

Notes 81

About The Author. 85

Acknowledgments

To Jesus Christ: my Rock, my Fortress and my Deliverer.

To the men and women of our steadfast law enforcement Bible study group, who have been constant inspirations to me—thank you. May God continue to protect and guide you.

To my pastors and teachers: thank you for your unwavering examples and love for Jesus.

To my wife for painstakingly reading, editing and keeping my focus on You, the Author and Finisher of our faith.

What Does God Say About Today's Law Enforcement Officer?

Introduction

- Have you ever wondered what God says about today's law enforcement officers?
- Is the job of a law enforcement officer mentioned in the Bible?
- Does the Bible allow a law enforcement officer to use force?
- Is it a heinous sin if a law enforcement officer takes the life of another?
- Does the Bible offer any encouragement or direction for today's law enforcement officers?
- Is the job of the law enforcement officer just an occupation or a calling?

In the United States of America, there are 780,000 law enforcement officers (deputy sheriffs, police officers, sergeants, lieutenants, captains, border patrol agents, marine officers, game wardens, etc.)[1], 469,500 correctional officers[2] and 90,000 probation/parole officers.[3]

In this book, it is my sincere hope every law enforcement officer will be encouraged and blessed to know his or her chosen profession was established by God.

May they gain greater confidence and determination, knowing the line-of-duty tasks they perform are those of peacemakers, sanctioned and condoned by the God of the universe.

Perhaps this book might, one day, fall into the hands of someone who has had a distasteful police encounter, or who has, for years, harbored an unfavorable opinion of those in law enforcement. May he or she, likewise, gain a new understanding, appreciation and respect for the God-ordained job of the law enforcement officer.

---

[1] http://www.bls.gov/ooh/protective-service/police-and-detectives.htm

[2] http://www.bls.gov/ooh/protective-service/correctional-officers.htm

[3] http://www.bls.gov/ooh/community-and-social-service/probation-officers-and-correctional-treatment-specialists.htm

CHAPTER 1
God's Job Description Of The Law Enforcement Officer

About two thousand years ago, the apostle Paul was often handcuffed (chained) to Roman soldiers (the law enforcement officer of his day) and, no doubt, saw firsthand how the local law enforcement officers performed their duties. In his letter to the Romans, he clearly taught that everyone was to obey his or her government—unless it violated God's Word.[4]

He wrote:

> "Obey the government, for God is the one who has put it there. There is no government anywhere that God has

---
[4] Acts 5:29

not placed in power. So those who refuse to obey the laws of the land are refusing to obey God, and punishment will follow.

For the policeman does not frighten people who are doing right; but those doing evil will always fear him. So if you don't want to be afraid, keep the laws and you will get along well. The policeman is sent by God to help you. But if you are doing something wrong, of course you should be afraid, for he will have you punished. He is sent by God for that very purpose. Obey the laws, then, for two reasons: first, to keep from being punished, and second, just because you know you should. Pay your taxes too, for these same two reasons. For government workers need to be paid so that they can keep on doing God's work, serving you. Pay everyone whatever he ought to have: pay your taxes and import duties gladly, obey those over you, and give honor and respect to all those to whom it is due," (Romans 13:1-7 TLB).

In North America, Europe and abroad, most local, state, provincial and/or federal governments have a modern political leadership structure which may include varying levels of elected and appointed officials. To support the citizens in their communities, officials may create a variety of services such as street maintenance, building safety, parks and recreation, library, fire protection and law enforcement services.

Once those services have been established, jobs will be filled by those in their community of which one of those services will be that of the law enforcement officer.

Just as every Christian should strive to be a peacemaker,[5] we must recognize God established the specific job of the law enforcement officer to

---

[5] James 3:18; Matthew 5:9

protect each respective community. As a matter of fact, the Bible says that, "Blessed *are* the peacemakers [which includes today's law enforcement officers], for they shall be called sons of God."[6]

Remember, Paul said:

> ...the policeman does not frighten people who are doing right; but those doing evil will always fear him. So if you don't want to be afraid, keep the laws and you will get along well. The policeman is sent by God to help you. But if you are doing something wrong, of course you should be afraid, for he will have you punished. He is sent by God for that very purpose.[7]

The real job description of the law enforcement officer is that of a "protector" who never frightens anyone who is doing right. That's why when people

---

[6] Matthew 5:9 NKJV

[7] Romans 13:3-4 TLB

run from a law enforcement officer, their fear and flight speaks volumes to the cop on the street.

CHAPTER 2

How The Bible Permits Law Enforcement Officers To Do Their Job

Governmental leaders in the United States, Australia, Japan and countless other countries have been given authority by God to establish their own laws to keep peace and order. How do we know governments can create laws? Because the Bible says to:

> Obey the government, for God is the one who has put it there. There is no government anywhere that God has not placed in power. So those who refuse to obey the laws of the land are

refusing to obey God, and punishment will follow.[8]

Yes, God is the One who has established governments worldwide. He gave each the authority to manage and govern as it chooses—which may include the creation of occupations to meet the needs of their community: in this case the peacemaker, better known as a law enforcement officer. The Living Bible uses the term "police officer", while in other translations, they are called *authorities* or *rulers*:[9]

> Therefore whoever resists the authority resists the ordinance of God, and those who resist will bring judgment on themselves. For rulers are not a terror to good works, but to evil."[10]

---

[8] Romans 13:1-2 TLB

[9] See NKJV or NLT

[10] Romans 13:2-3a NKJV

Therefore, within the context in which Paul is directing this letter, one can easily see there are varying levels of governmental "rulers" or "authorities", for which our focus will be primarily on the law enforcement officer.

Since we know each of these positions has been ordained by God, each respective governmental jurisdiction may thereby create laws and boundaries which every citizen (to include the law enforcement officer) must follow. For instance, in California, lawmakers implemented Penal Code section 830.1–830.3, which defines the types of peace officers and their duties—to include the police officer, marshal, sheriff, corrections, probation and parole officers, and a number of other specialized peace officer positions.[11] Lawmakers also enacted California Penal Code section 836 to give to law enforcement officers the power of arrest.[12] In order to make sure every law enforcement officer was properly trained, the California legislature

---

[11] http://www.leginfo.ca.gov/cgi-bin/displaycode?section=pen&group=00001-01000&file=830-832.17

[12] http://www.leginfo.ca.gov/cgi-bin/displaycode?section=pen&group=00001-01000&file=833-851.90

enacted specific training regulations in California Penal Code section 13510.[13] Not only in California are there specific laws governing the duties of law enforcement officers, but in New York, one can also find very similar provisions in the New York Criminal Code, sections 2.10–2.30.[14]

---

[13] http://www.leginfo.ca.gov/cgi-bin/displaycode?section=pen&group=13001-14000&file=13510-13519.15

[14] http://law.onecle.com/new-york/criminal-procedure/part1.ta.a2.html

CHAPTER 3

In What Manner May A Law Enforcement Officer Enforce The Laws?

Even though law enforcement officers in the United States have been granted authority to make arrests and issue summons and tickets, does that mean each officer can operate with impunity? Unequivocally, no. Every state and federal law enforcement officer in the United States must never intentionally, maliciously, or negligently harm another person. For instance, law enforcement officers can be prosecuted for violating their duties in California under Penal Code sections

422.6[15] or 149[16]; or, in Texas under Title 8, Chapter 39 of the Texas Penal Code.[17] The United States Government also may step in and charge officers with civil rights violations under Title 18, U.S. Code, Section 242 – Deprivation of Rights Under Color of Law.[18] By the way, did you know this United States code not only applies to law enforcement officers, but also to mayors, judges, council members, and even nursing home proprietors?

One of the greatest, and most effective, tools available to every law enforcement officer world-wide, to assist them in enforcing laws, comes in a very small enclosure—it is called the tongue. Every law enforcement officer who attends a modern training academy has been instructed to use the art of negotiation before escalating to varying levels of force. As every law enforcement officer knows (or will one day discover), there are times when he

---

[15] http://www.leginfo.ca.gov/cgi-bin/displaycode?section=pen&group=00001-01000&file=422.6-422.865

[16] http://www.leginfo.ca.gov/cgi-bin/displaycode?section=pen&group=00001-01000&file=142-181

[17] http://www.statutes.legis.state.tx.us/Docs/PE/htm/PE.39.htm

[18] http://www.justice.gov/crt/about/crm/242fin.php

or she has no choice but to immediately use less lethal or deadly force. Even with continuous annual, mandated, advanced officer training updates for law enforcement officers, there will always be unusual circumstances and incidents for which a law enforcement officer will encounter that are "out of the box". Whatever situation arises in which a law enforcement officer must enforce the law, every decision they make will, in some form, be based on the following: governmental laws, departmental policies and procedures, training (overshadowed with common sense), and combined with an ethical and moral compass.

CHAPTER 4
Does The Bible Give Law Enforcement Officers Authority To Do Their Job?

To answer that question, let's look at what's written in the Bible, as it pertains to citizens and their governments:

> Be subject for the Lord's sake to every human institution, whether it be to the emperor as supreme, or to governors as sent by him to punish those who do evil and to praise those who do good.[19]

---

[19] 1 Peter 2:13 ESV

> Remind them to be submissive to rulers and authorities, to be obedient, to be ready for every good work.[20]
>
> Let every person be subject to the governing authorities. For there is no authority except from God, and those that exist have been instituted by God.[21]

Plainly stated, no matter where or who you are, the Bible says the laws created by each respective governmental entity are to be obeyed. Paul also wrote that, "...Therefore whoever resists the authorities resists what God has appointed, and those who resist will incur judgment."[22]

Even though law enforcement officers have been given authority to do their jobs, it's important they remember their position as a deputy sheriff, police officer, detective, constable or special agent,

---

[20] Titus 3:1 ESV

[21] Romans 13:1 ESV

[22] Romans 13:2 ESV

etc., has been designed *to serve* (the people) and not to *be served* (by the people). Yes, whenever a law enforcement officer writes a ticket, arrests a drunk driver, resolves a domestic dispute, or takes a bicycle theft report, he or she is doing his/her job, serving the people, as outlined in the Bible. Remember, Paul said, "...government workers need to be paid so that they can keep on doing God's work, serving you."[23] The Bible clearly says the law enforcement officer is to be a servant to his or her community, city, county, state, or nation.

---

[23] Romans 13:6 ESV

CHAPTER 5

The Law Enforcement Officer And The Use Of Less Lethal Types Of Force

Now that we've established the Bible allows governments to create jobs for public service, such as a judge or law enforcement officer, governments may also establish laws to maintain peace and order, particularly for those who resist the authorities.

In California, if someone resists arrest, California Penal Code section 835a permits a law enforcement officer to, "use reasonable force to effect the arrest, to prevent escape or to overcome resistance".[24] In New York, Penal Code section 35.30

---

[24] http://www.leginfo.ca.gov/cgi-bin/displaycode?section=pen&group=00001-01000&file=833-851.90

provides similar language and authority for New York law enforcement officers.[25]

Let's look again at what Paul wrote. He said:

> Let every soul be subject to the governing authorities. For there is no authority except from God, and the authorities that exist are appointed by God. Therefore whoever resists the authority resists the ordinance of God, and those who resist will bring judgment on themselves.[26]

Even though federal, state, and local laws have been established to allow law enforcement officers to "use reasonable force to effect the arrest, to prevent escape or to overcome resistance," many law enforcement agencies have enacted policies and procedures outlining the extent to which their law enforcement officers may use reasonable force to

---

[25] http://codes.lp.findlaw.com/nycode/PEN/ONE/C/35/35.30

[26] Romans 13:1-2 NKJV

effect the arrest. In order to effectively equip law enforcement officers to make the right choices and decisions to effect the arrest, they are also required by law to attend a certified training academy to learn the most current tactics and procedures.

Just as citizens are subject to the governing authorities, law enforcement officers must follow their respective federal, state, and local laws, to include their departmental policies and procedures as well. If a law enforcement officer should deviate from any of those laws, policies, or procedures, he/she may be prosecuted and/or be subjected to discipline or termination.

As previously mentioned, the law enforcement officer is:

> God's minister to you for good. But if you do evil, be afraid; for he does not bear the sword [weapon] in vain; for he is God's minister, an avenger to execute wrath on him who practices evil.[27]

---
[27] Romans 13:4 NKJV

If a law enforcement officer uses any weapon in vain (contrary to laws, policies, and procedures; or with malice, negligence, and/or intent to harm), he or she has not only violated God's word, but may also be subject to prosecution under state, federal, or local laws.

That leads us to this question—does the Bible allow a law enforcement officer to use a baton, control holds, less lethal devices, or other physical uses of force?

We need to look again at what Paul said:

> For he [the law enforcement officer] is God's minister to you for good. But if you do evil, be afraid; for he does not bear the sword [weapon] in vain; for he is God's minister [servant], an avenger to execute wrath on him who practices evil.[28]

In Paul's time, he was frequently shackled to a Roman soldier and became keenly aware of the

---
[28] Romans 13:4 NKJV

tools and clothing that identified them as soldiers—much like the uniform and badge worn by today's law enforcement officer. So why would Paul write that the soldier does not "bear the sword [weapon] in vain"? Every Roman soldier usually carried three weapons: a dagger for very close fighting, a sword for fighting a person from a few feet away, and a javelin for longer distance combat. Every soldier carried those weapons for defensive, as well as offensive, purposes.[29]

The weapons today's law enforcement officers carry—those for very close defensive or offensive encounters, or for those nearby or farther away—are only to be used to effect an arrest, to prevent escape, or to overcome resistance. For a close, resistive encounter, an officer might use control holds or a collapsible "Asp" baton. For a resistive encounter a few feet away, an officer might use the extended "Asp" baton, pepper spray, Taser, or even a handgun, if his/her life or the life of another was

---

[29] http://www.bbc.co.uk/schools/primaryhistory/romans/the_roman_army/ AND http://www.tribunesandtriumphs.org/roman-weapons/weapons-of-the-roman-soldiers.htm

in danger. If there was a threat at a longer distance, an officer might use a Taser, shotgun, or rifle.

The key to what Paul said was the fact, "[the law enforcement officer] does not bear the sword [weapon] in vain." Vain can be translated "without reason or without cause".[30] In this case, the "sword" of today's law enforcement officer may include the use of control holds, baton, pepper spray, Taser, firearm, less lethal devices, or using his/her police cruiser as a tool; plus other available offensive/defensive equipment.

So, as the government allowed the Roman soldier to carry and use varying weapons for offensive and defensive purposes, the Bible vicariously allows law enforcement officers to use modern-day equipment to accomplish their mission, in accordance with laws, policies, and procedures.

---

[30] Strong's Hebrew and Greek Dictionary (Reference G1500)

CHAPTER 6

The Law Enforcement Officer And The Use Of Deadly Force

The Bible says:

> ... if you are doing something wrong, of course you should be afraid, for he [the law enforcement officer] will have you punished. He is sent by God for that very purpose.[31]

Whenever a law enforcement officer uses ANY form of force, he or she must remember his or her PRIMARY task must be ONLY to take the person into custody, and cause that violator to be taken before a court of law. That law enforcement officer must NEVER *cause* the punishment, but

---
[31] Romans 13:4 TLB

bring the violator before a judge, who will render the punishment in a court of law.

That takes us to the ultimate question—can a law enforcement officer use deadly force?

As we just established, the job of a law enforcement officer is to "BRING" a violator before a court of law, where a judge will mete out the punishment. Since law enforcement officers have been given the authority to "BRING" a violator before a judge, they have also been given the discretionary latitude to use the necessary tools at their disposal to accomplish that task. Of course one of those tools, the firearm, may be used to accomplish that goal.

Let's pause to look at the laws of California and New York for a moment. California Penal Code section 197[32] and New York Penal Code section 35.30[33] both allow deadly force to be used by a peace officer, under a multitude of circumstances and situations. In these pages, it would be virtually impossible to specifically state when, and under what

---

[32] http://www.leginfo.ca.gov/cgi-bin/displaycode?section=pen&group=00001-01000&file=187-199

[33] http://ypdcrime.com/penal.law/article35.htm#p35.30

circumstances, a law enforcement officer may be legally authorized to use deadly force. Nonetheless, since the Bible allows governments to create jobs, they may establish laws outlining the legal use of deadly force as we've just seen.

Since law enforcement officers have been biblically allowed to use deadly force, following the guidelines of Romans 13, have you ever wondered how a law enforcement officer, who must use deadly force and take a life, resolves the commandment, "Thou shall not kill"?[34] Every law enforcement officer should know that particular commandment is actually translated, "Thou shalt not murder". The Hebrew word for "murder" literally means, "The intentional, premeditated killing of another person *with malice.*"[35]

Finally, if a law enforcement officer uses a firearm and is forced to take the life of another, the Bible clearly teaches that such law enforcement officer was acting as an agent of the government, which was established by God. As long as

---

[34] Exodus 20:13 KJV

[35] Strong's Hebrew and Greek Dictionary (Reference H7523)

the officer acted in accordance with their existing laws; in accordance with their established policies; harbored no malice or intent to harm another; was not negligent; and acted in harmony with Romans 13:4, where it was his or her intent to "bring" the violator before a magistrate to be punished, then that law enforcement officer acted as a genuine peacemaker following the biblical precepts. Remember, "Blessed are the peacemakers, for they shall be called the sons of God."[36]

---

[36] Matthew 5:9 NKJV

CHAPTER 7

The Law Enforcement Officer – An Occupation Or A Calling?

Why will only a small percentage of applicants successfully pass the rigorous screening process and become a law enforcement officer? Could it be those who pass have an innate ability to handle the rigors of the job? For instance, how many people do you know who are great painters of art, while others can only draw stick figures? What about a family in which several siblings are athletic, non-athletic, or intellectual? Or, how about well-known professional sports figures whose children follow in their mother or father's footsteps?

Everyone has a gift, ability, or talent to do something—such as working with youth, repairing things, raising children, politics, etc. If someone discovers he/she has a desire to become a law enforcement officer, and makes it through the screening process, it is very likely he/she has discovered his/her God-given talent—especially after graduating an academy and working on the street.

Ultimately, how does someone know he/she has been called to be a law enforcement officer?

It's when he/she finds:

- He/she has an abundance of patience;
- An inquisitive mind;
- A desire for justice;
- A willingness to help others;
- An ability to cope with danger and death; and
- Wants to do what's right.

It is when he or she realizes he/she possesses those traits that he/she was very likely called to be, "…God's servant, an agent of wrath to bring punishment on the wrongdoer."[37]

---

[37] Romans 13:4b NIV

CHAPTER 8

Will Every Law Enforcement Officer Automatically Get Into Heaven?

No! Just as your decision to become a law enforcement officer was a personal decision, everyone must also make an individual choice to accept the way God chose for each person to gain eternal life. Should you choose not to receive the salvation that has been provided by the Son of God, your rejection will cause you to spend eternity away from God, after death, in a place called hell. On the other hand, if you'd like to know how to avoid that horrific destination, then go to the appendix at the back of the book.

CHAPTER 9

So, What Does God Really Say About Today's Law Enforcement Officer?

Ever since the first recorded crime in the Bible (when Cain killed his brother, Abel),[38] communities across the globe have been in need of protection. To keep order and peace, God established governments and allowed each to implement plans to protect and support their citizens. The occupation most notably at the forefront that protects citizens worldwide (excluding the military), has become known as the law enforcement officer or the peacemaker.

Here's why God created the job of a law enforcement officer:

---

[38] Genesis 4:8

- Because He knew there would be those who would "resist...the authority"...and..."bring judgment on themselves."[39]

- Not to be "a terror to [citizen's with] good conduct, but to [those with] bad [conduct]."[40]

- To be God's servant for [every citizen's] good.[41]

- To let those who do wrong know they are to "be afraid, for he [the law enforcement officer] does not bear the sword [his/her weapons and tools] in vain. For he is the servant of God, an avenger who carries out God's wrath on the wrongdoer."[42]

---

[39] Romans 13:2 ESV

[40] Romans 13:3 ESV

[41] Romans 13:4a ESV

[42] Romans 13:4b ESV

- So the wrongdoers will know they are to be, "…[in] subjection [to the law enforcement officer], not only to avoid God's wrath but also for the sake of conscience."[43]

If you are a law enforcement officer, may you know the profession you've chosen is one of nobility, created by our Most High God to keep lawlessness in check. As you do your job as a peacemaker, may God pour out His wisdom upon your hands, your mind, your heart, your soul, and your feet.

Until Jesus returns to establish worldwide peace, God will continue to use peacemakers, because there will always be peace-breakers and peace-takers. So, in all aspects of your duties, remember to do so with **I**ntegrity, **R**esponsibility, **O**bedience, and **N**obility. In everything you do, be that "I.R.O.N cop" for Jesus.

---

[43] Romans 13:5 ESV

Biblical Encouragement For Christian Law Enforcement Officers

God's guide for every law enforcement officer to do his/her job:

Let your conduct be without covetousness; be content with such things as you have. For He Himself has said, "I will never leave you nor forsake you." So we may boldly say: "The Lord is my helper; I will not fear. What can man do to me?" (Hebrews 13:5-6 NKJV)

So do not fear, for I am with you; do not be dismayed, for I am your God. I will strengthen you and help you; I will uphold you with my righteous right hand. (Isaiah 41:10 NIV)

God is our refuge and strength, an ever-present help in trouble. (Psalm 46:1 NIV)

Do not take revenge, my friends, but leave room for God's wrath, for it is written: "It is mine to avenge; I will repay," says the Lord. (Romans 12:19 NIV)

Trust in the LORD with all your heart and lean not on your own understanding; in all your ways acknowledge him, and he will make your paths straight. (Proverbs 3:5-6 NIV)

It is God who arms me with strength and makes my way perfect. (Psalm 18:32 NIV)

Instruct a wise man and he will be wiser still; teach a righteous man and he will add to his learning. (Proverbs 9:9 NIV)

This is how the Lord watches over the law enforcement officer:

But You, O Lord, are a shield for me, My glory and the One who lifts up my head. I cried to the Lord with my voice, And He heard me from His holy hill. (Psalm 3:3-4 NKJV)

As for God, his way is perfect; the word of the LORD is flawless. He is a shield for all who take refuge in him. (Psalm 18:30 NIV)

So we say with confidence, The Lord is my helper; I will not be afraid. What can man do to me? (Hebrews 13:6 NIV)

> Have I not commanded you? Be strong and courageous. Do not be terrified; do not be discouraged, for the LORD your God will be with you wherever you go. (Joshua 1:9 NIV)

> He will call upon me, and I will answer him; I will be with him in trouble, I will deliver him and honor him. (Psalm 91:15 NIV)

God wants the law enforcement officer to act professionally and protect others, as follows:

> Speak up for those who cannot speak for themselves; ensure justice for those being crushed. (Proverbs 31:8 NLT)

> And whatever you do, do it heartily, as to the Lord and not to men... (Colossians 3:23 NKJV)

And whatever you do, in word or deed, do everything in the name of the Lord Jesus, giving thanks to God the Father through him. (Colossians 3:17 NIV)

Therefore, whether you eat or drink, or whatever you do, do all to the glory of God. (1 Corinthians 10:31 NKJV)

Bless those who persecute you; bless and do not curse them. Rejoice with those who rejoice, weep with those who weep. Live in harmony with one another. Do not be haughty, but associate with the lowly. Never be wise in your own sight. Repay no one evil for evil, but give thought to do what is honorable in the sight of all. If possible, so far as it depends on you, live peaceably with all... (Romans 12:14-21 ESV)

God's Word will encourage the law enforcement officer through difficult times:

I have told you these things, so that in me you may have peace. In this world you will have trouble. But take heart! I have overcome the world. (John 16:33 NIV)

Be still, and know that I am God. (Psalm 46:10 NKJV)

And we know that all things work together for good to those who love God, to those who are the called according to His purpose. (Romans 8:28 NKJV)

Therefore do not worry, saying, "What shall we eat?" Or "What shall we drink?" Or "What shall we wear?" For after all these things the Gentiles seek. For your heavenly Father knows that you need all these things. But seek first the kingdom of God and His righteousness, and all these things shall be added to you. Therefore do not worry about tomorrow... (Matthew 6:31-34 NKJV)

Be gracious to me, O God, be gracious to me, For my soul takes refuge in You; And in the shadow of Your wings I will take refuge until destruction passes by. I will cry to God Most High, To God who accomplishes all things for me. He will send from heaven and save me; He reproaches him who tramples upon me. God will send forth His lovingkindness and His truth. (Psalm 57:1-3 NASB)

Cast your cares on the LORD and he will sustain you; he will never let the righteous fall. (Psalm 55:22 NIV)

Humble yourselves, therefore, under God's mighty hand, that he may lift you up in due time. Cast all your anxiety on him because he cares for you. (1 Peter 5:6-7 NIV)

Remember the oath of office you took to be a law enforcement officer:

If a man makes a vow to the Lord, or swears an oath to bind himself by some agreement, he shall not break his word; he shall do according to all that proceeds out of his mouth. (Numbers 30:2 NKJV)

Fear the LORD your God, serve him only and take your oaths in his name. (Deuteronomy 6:13 NIV)

I say, "Keep the king's commandment for the sake of your oath to God. Do not be hasty to go from his presence.

Do not take your stand for an evil thing"... (Ecclesiastes 8:2-3a)

Fear the LORD your God and serve him. Hold fast to him and take your oaths in his name. (Deuteronomy 10:20 NIV)

Stay away from the love of money; be satisfied with what you have. For God has said, "I will never fail you. I will never forsake you." (Hebrews 13:5 NLT)

Blessed is the man who does not walk in the counsel of the wicked or stand in the way of sinners or sit in the seat of mockers. But his delight is in the law of the LORD, and on his law he meditates day and night. (Psalm 1:1-2 NIV)

Wise Sayings For Cops

by Randy Emon

Trust your sidearm, trust your instinct, trust your training, trust your wit...
...Above all, trust in the Lord.

"I solemnly swear to tell the truth, the whole truth and nothing but the truth so help me God."
So, what does embellishing mean again?

As lights and sirens announce an emergency...
...Guilt and shame can do the same.

To "Protect and Serve" is a noble goal...
...To "Trust and Obey" is the better way.

TASER darts will pierce the skin...
...But pesky sins go deep within.

Batons can break bones...
...Reckless words can break hearts.

Calling 911 and being placed on hold...
...is like praying with willful sin in your heart.

A foul-mouthed cop and a rotten apple...
...both leave a bad taste.

"I want ripped muscles, an 80" HDTV,
a boat, and a bigger house."
How about, "...give us this day our daily bread"?

An officer survival course can
keep a cop sharp...
...so can a Bible study.

Lightweight, durable boots are an invaluable
resource for every cop...
...so is a friend who sticks closer than a brother.

Your department may arm you with weapons...
...but God arms you with His strength.

As every law enforcement officer knows the value
of "master grip"...
...I wonder how many know the value of being in
the Master's Grip?

Road flares warn drivers of danger, provide illumination, and create a safety zone...

...So does the Holy Spirit.

"Ready on the right, ready on the left, ready on the firing line."

So, that's how you defend the Faith!

There are lots of sergeants,

lieutenants, and captains...

...but there's only ONE Rock,

Fortress, and Deliverer.

Robbery suspects might say,

"Give me everything."

But God says, "You can't give ME anything until you've given ME everything."

Wearing a uniform will not make you a cop...
...any more than sitting in a church will make you a Christian.

As a cop guards suspects...
...don't forget to guard your heart.

When you retire as a cop, will you be remembered for how many arrests you made, how many tickets you wrote or...
...how many games of Candyland and Yahtzee you played with your kids?

A weapon without bullets
is ineffective and powerless...
...so is the cop who lacks integrity and honor.

What do you call a cop who goes home after work, and not out with the guys?
Faithful and trustworthy!

What do you call a cop who says,
"I don't need any help, I can do it myself"?
Does "FOOL" come to mind?

A Prayer For Today's Law Enforcement Officer

Dear Lord, as law enforcement officers, we thank you that You are Wonderful, that You are our Counselor, our Mighty God, our Everlasting Father, and our Prince of Peace. We, as law enforcement officers, thank you, Lord, for the privilege to be used as Your instruments of righteousness, to serve every person in America—regardless of their background or heritage. Lord, every day, nearly one million men and women protect more than 300 million Americans from tyranny, anarchy, crime, danger, and evil... And at every moment, these law enforcement officers are in the midst of peril, wherever they travel—on the roads, in the cities, in the wilderness, on the local waters, and even while they are eating their lunches. Danger lurks at every corner. The loss of just one officer,

Lord, is too much to bear at any time, yet there are thousands of officers across America who (even right now) will encounter shootings, fights, pursuits, ambushes, evil, and danger. Lord, we are so grateful that Your Word has acknowledged that when a man or woman becomes a law enforcement officer, he/she has accepted a divine appointment from YOU to serve the people of his/her community, state, or country. So, Lord, as law enforcement officers, we come to ask Your blessings and mercy upon us. We ask for Your hands of love to grip us; Your arms of strength to embrace us; Your legs of might to uphold us; Your eyes of kindness to watch us; and Your mind of infinite wisdom to guide us. May every law enforcement officer in America know his/her job has been established by You and that whatever he/she does, and wherever he/she goes, may he/she sense Your presence, even in the midst of difficult circumstances. More than anything, Lord, for those officers, deputies, agents, or investigators who do not know You personally, may Your Holy Spirit sweetly settle upon them on-duty, off-duty, or wherever they go. May You draw them

A Prayer For Today's Law Enforcement Officer

close to Your heart, where there is endless mercy and grace. May you give every Christian officer in America increased boldness to share Your love with their co-workers. Your word says the angels rejoice in heaven whenever one person repents, so, Lord, may You grant opportunities for many officers to receive Jesus Christ into their hearts, to be their Savior and Lord, and receive eternal life. May You be with the wives, husbands, children, brothers, sisters, parents, friends, fiancés, boyfriends, or girlfriends of every law enforcement officer; and grant them grace to support and encourage each law enforcement officer through the difficult days that have passed, and of those that will come in the future. May You be with the heart, spirit, soul, and mind of every law enforcement officer who has had to endure horrendous tragedy and may You, Lord, forever protect them from any future emotional trauma. May they know, without a doubt, You will never leave them nor forsake them, for You will always be their Shield and their Strong Tower against all enemies. This we ask in the precious and glorious name of Jesus Christ. Amen.

Appendix

How to Avoid Eternity in Hell and Receive Eternal Life:

If you've intentionally turned to this page, rest assured it was not by accident. I would not be surprised that as you started to read this, your cellphone rang, a dirty joke came to your mind, you suddenly felt hungry, or your vision got blurred. Hold on, because what you're about to read will be better than a high-speed pursuit or a good felony arrest and, most of all, will last an eternity.

By the way, if you're pressed for time and have a computer or cellphone, just go to this web address and check it out there: http://ironguys.org/how_to_become_a_Christian.html

Or read on:

Step 1:
God's Purpose: Peace and Life
The Bible Says:

"..we have peace with God through our Lord Jesus Christ." (Romans 5:1 NKJV)

"For God so loved the world that He gave His only begotten Son, that whoever believes in Him should not perish but have everlasting life." (John 3:16 NKJV)

"...I have come that they may have life, and that they may have it more abundantly." (John 10:10b NKJV)

Step 2:
Our Problem: Separation
The Bible says:

"For all have sinned and fall short of the glory of God." (Romans 3:23 NKJV)

"For the wages of sin is death, but the gift of God is eternal life in Christ Jesus our Lord." (Romans 6:23 NKJV)

"There is a way that seems right to man, but in the end it leads to death." (Proverbs 14:12 NIV)

"But your iniquities have separated you from God; and your sins have hidden His face from you, so that He will not hear." (Isaiah 59:2 NKJV)

Step 3:
God's Remedy: The Cross
The Bible Says:

"...God is on one side and all the people on the other side, and Christ Jesus,

Himself man, is between them to bring them together..." (1 Timothy 2:5 TLB)

"For Christ also has suffered once for sins, the just for the unjust, that He might bring us to God..." (1 Peter 3:18a NIV)

"But God demonstrates His own love for us in this: While we were still sinners, Christ died for us." (Romans 5:8)

Step 4:
Our Response: Receive Christ
The Bible Says:

"Behold, I stand at the door and knock. If anyone hears my voice and opens the door, I will come in to him and dine with him, and he with Me." (Revelation 3:20 NKJV)

"But as many as received Him, to them He gave the right to become children of God, even to those who believe in His name." (John 1:12 NASB)

"...if you confess with your mouth the Lord Jesus and believe in your heart that God has raised Him from the dead, you will be saved." (Romans 10:9 NKJV)

Is there any good reason why you cannot receive Jesus Christ right now?

Then pray this following prayer to receive Him as Lord and Savior:

Dear Lord Jesus, I know that I am a sinner and need Your forgiveness. I believe that You died for my sins. I want to turn from my sins and confess all of my sins to You. I now invite You to come into my heart and life. Fill me with Your Holy Spirit. Take control of my life, and make me the person You want me to be. I want to trust and follow You as Lord and Savior. In the name of Jesus Christ. Amen.

God's Assurance: His Word

The Bible Says:

"For whoever calls upon the name of the Lord will be saved." (Romans 10:13 NASB)

"For it is by grace you have been saved, through faith–and this is not from yourselves, it is the gift of God–not by works, so that no one can boast." (Ephesians 2:8-9 NIV)

"He who has the Son has life: he who does not have the Son of God does not have life. These things I have written to you who believe in the name of the Son of God, that you may know that you have eternal life, and that you may continue to believe in the name of the Son of God." (1 John 5:12-13 NKJV)

Notes

Notes

Notes

Notes

About The Author

Randy Emon has been in law enforcement forty-three years—the first twenty-three years as a sergeant with the Baldwin Park (California) Police Department. Currently, he is a supervising deputy coroner investigator with the San Bernardino County (California) Sheriff-Coroner.

Randy and his wife, Lora, have been married forty years, and have two sons and a daughter who are also law enforcement officers in Southern California.

In 2010, Randy founded IronGuys Law Enforcement Ministries (www.Ironguys.org) to support the men and women of law enforcement, and leads a monthly law enforcement Bible study.

You may contact Randy by email at Randy@Ironguys.org.

www.ingramcontent.com/pod-product-compliance
Ingram Content Group UK Ltd.
Pitfield, Milton Keynes, MK11 3LW, UK
UKHW022217230426
12048UKWH00016BA/891